The Death of the Dinosaurs

written by Herbie Brennan

illustrated by Chris Brown, Andrew Warrington
and James Sneddon

Contents

Introduction

Dinosaurs first appeared on Earth more than 200 million years ago. For most of that time these enormous animals roamed throughout the world.

They were the kings of this planet. Humans, who appeared much later, are just four million years old at the most.

Dinosaurs had no natural enemies. Yet, 65 million years ago, they disappeared.

The big question is **why?**

There are two main theories about what happened to the dinosaurs. Scientists have been arguing about theories for years:

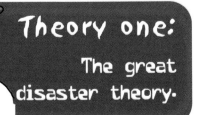

Theory one:
The great disaster theory.

Theory two:
The slow death theory.

The great disaster theory

This is what some scientists believe:

A giant lump of rock, or **meteor**, from outer space crashed into the Earth about 65 million years ago.

The crash was so violent that it left
a huge dent (called a **crater**) on the
surface of the Earth.

When something like that
happens, huge amounts
of dirt and dust are
thrown high up
into the air.

There was so much dust that it blocked out the light and heat of the Sun for many months, perhaps even years.

Without sunlight, plants could no longer grow.

Some dinosaurs ate plants.
They needed tons of plants
each day, so they died first
when the plants disappeared.

As the plant-eating dinosaurs died,
the meat-eaters who hunted them
had less and less to eat.

The dust cleared at last and the Sun shone again, but by then it was too late for the dinosaurs. They had all starved to death.

It might have happened even faster than that. Some scientists believe dinosaurs were cold-blooded and needed sunshine to warm them up. If this was so, they would have died from the cold even before the food ran out.

Fossil skeletons tell us about the dinosaurs that died.

8

Evidence for the great disaster theory

What evidence do scientists have for this theory?

When scientists dug down to what was the surface of the Earth 65 million years ago, they found

Iridium was found in this small meteor.

a layer of metal called **iridium**. Iridium is very rare on the Earth's surface. It is much more common in rocks in outer space.

So scientists think that the iridium must have been part of a meteor that crashed into the Earth.

Scientists also found a type of brittle rock, called **quartz**, at the same level as the iridium. The quartz had cracks in it. The cracks were the sort you would expect to find if something struck the Earth very hard.

A close-up photo of cracked quartz.

Scientists also discovered lots of glass beads that they thought had been formed in the explosion when the meteor struck the Earth.

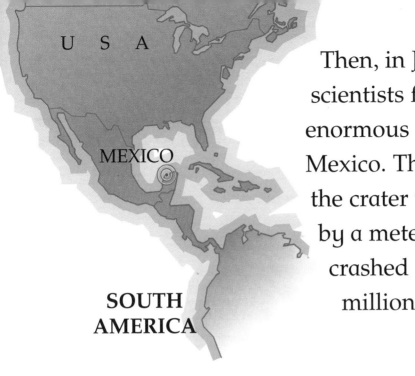

U S A

MEXICO

SOUTH
AMERICA

Then, in June 1990, scientists found an enormous crater in Mexico. They believe the crater was made by a meteor that crashed to Earth 65 million years ago.

The slow death theory

However, some scientists believe another theory.

This is what they believe:

At the time the dinosaurs appeared on Earth, there was only one enormous stretch of land on the whole planet. The dinosaurs roamed across almost every part of it.

This enormous land mass, called Pangaea, existed over 200 million years ago.

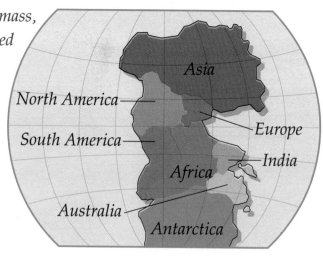

North America

South America

Asia

Europe

India

Africa

Australia

Antarctica

But over millions of
years, this great mass of
land started to break up
very slowly.

During the break-up, **volcanoes** erupted
and sea levels rose and fell. The weather
changed. The world had been hot, but
now it turned cold.

All this brought changes in the type of plants that could grow and the sort of animals that could live on Earth.

The dinosaurs could not cope
with their new surroundings.

The number of dinosaurs slowly got
smaller. At last they died out altogether.

Evidence for the slow death theory

What evidence do scientists have
for this theory?

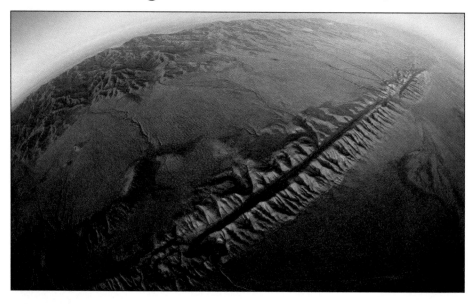

*This crack in the Earth shows where
two continents are moving apart*

Scientists now know that all the **continents**
of the world are moving apart very,
very slowly.

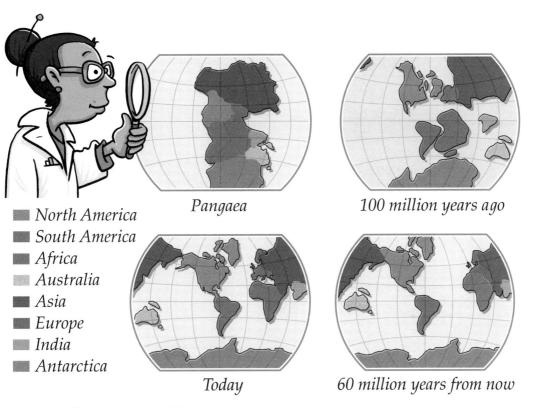

North America
South America
Africa
Australia
Asia
Europe
India
Antarctica

Pangaea

100 million years ago

Today

60 million years from now

The break-up of Pangaea

They can tell that there was once a time
when all the continents were pressed
together in one great mass of land.
If you look at a world map today, you
can see how well Africa once fitted
up against North America and South
America, like pieces of a jigsaw puzzle.

fossils found on high land

sea

Fossils of sea creatures have been found on high land and low land. This shows that the sea levels rose and fell millions of years ago.

Fossil of a fish

Scientists have studied layers of melted rock, called **lava**, that is produced when volcanoes erupt. The lava shows that many volcanoes must have erupted at the time that the dinosaurs disappeared.

Lava flowing from a volcano

Which theory is right?

A problem for scientists is that the same evidence can be used to support both the great disaster theory and the slow death theory.

A meteor crashing into the Earth will produce glass beads, iridium, and cracks in quartz.

Volcanoes erupting will also produce glass beads, bring up iridium from deep inside the Earth, and cause cracks in quartz.

21

In the years ahead, scientists might find evidence for a new theory. Perhaps they will find evidence that will settle the matter once and for all. But until they do, the argument continues.

Glossary

continents the main masses of land on the Earth's surface

crater a bowl-shaped hole made by a meteor crashing into the Earth

dinosaurs animals, now extinct, which lived on Earth over 65 million years ago

iridium a metal found deep inside the Earth and in objects from space, but rarely on the Earth's surface

lava melted rock flowing from a volcano

meteor a rock from space

quartz a type of crystal rock

volcano an opening in the Earth's surface. Lava pours through it onto the Earth's surface

Index